SIDEPRENEUR

CREATING A LIFE WHILE MAKING A LIVING

**Your Path to Creating MORE MONEY,
MORE TIME and MORE OPTIONS
While Working Your Day Job**

RIK COVALINSKI

To purchase copies of this book in bulk at a discount or have the author speak at your event, please contact Rik Covalinski at rik.covalinski@gmail.com.

Sidepreneur: Creating a Life While Making a Living
Your Path to Creating More Money, More Time and More Options While Working Your Day Job
Copyright © 2020 RIK COVALINSKI. All rights reserved.
Published by RIK COVALINSKI
ISBN: 978-1-71679-903-7 (print)
ISBN: 978-1-71674-429-7 (ebook)
The above information forms this copyright notice: © 2020 by RIK COVALINSKI.
All rights reserved.

Library of Congress Control Number: 2020912842

Description: Whether we like it or not the days of working in a long-term career for one company and retiring comfortably is a thing of the past. Too many people are tired of running in a rat race only to find themselves living paycheck to paycheck. More than ever employees are actively searching for a way to get ahead. They can't see themselves working for 40 years with little to nothing to show for it. They want to step out of the life of average to create more money, more time and more options for them and their family. "Sidepreneur: Creating a Life While Making a Living" was written for the genuinely ambitious seeking that change. They know these times are full of potential and are wanting to have a business of their own, but they don't know where to start. They can't afford to quit their jobs to invest all their time and money into a new venture. The answer is to become an entrepreneur on the side; a Sidepreneur! Readers will find a path for taking their unproductive time outside of their job and investing it into a side business of their own.

Cover Design: uniquebookcover.com
Page Design: MindtheMargins.com

DEDICATION

I dedicate this book first to my parents who, from a young age supported and encouraged me to follow my dreams. Secondly, I want to dedicate this book to my family who, through the bad times and good have always believed in me and partnered with me in creating a legacy. Finally, I wouldn't be where I am now without the numerous mentors I've had pour into my life.

FACT: The average debt of a household is over $25,000

"…Americans who carry debt, a third (33%) of their monthly income goes toward paying it off, exclusive of mortgages. Those with debt report having $26,621 on average, and 13% of Americans expect to be in debt the rest of their lives."[1]

1. www.news.northwesternmutual.com/planning-and-progress-2020

FACT: Fewer people can save what they need for retirement

"Millennials should aim to set aside nearly half of their income for the future…"[2]

2. www.cnbc.com/2019/10/23/millennials-need-to-save-an-huge-percent-of-paycheck-to-retire-at-65

FACT: The fund for the U.S. Social Security is being depleted

"Your estimated benefits are based on current law. The law governing benefit amounts may change because the combined trust fund reserves are projected to become depleted by 2035 — the same as projected last year. Payroll taxes collected will be enough to pay only about 79 cents for each dollar of scheduled benefits."[3]

3. www.ssa.gov/benefits/retirement/estimator

Did you catch that?
"…the combined trust fund reserves are projected to become depleted by 2035…"

As people are struggling with individual debt, not putting money into savings and not having a peace-of mind about their future, more and more people are not only wanting, but **needing** to create more money. They can't afford to quit their jobs to jump into a business of their own, so they turn to creating an income stream <u>on the side</u> of their jobs. They are wanting *more money*, *more options* and *more time*. They are becoming Sidepreneurs and creating a life while making a living!

FREE TOOLS & RESOURCES!

I have created additional tools that you can use as you read through this book. Many are mentioned throughout the reading, but I have added several extras for those who want a little more. They are posted online. Visit www.sidepreneurbook.com to register your book for access to these free resources.

CONTENTS

FOREWORD

Why I Wrote This Book

Do you feel stuck? Maybe you feel like you are not where you want to be in life, or you've been working at a job for several years and feel like you shouldn't be struggling so much. You've played by life's rules, but you are not where you want, or thought you should be. You see success all around you or on the Internet and ask, "why can't that be me" or "how can I do that?"

That was me several years ago. I had been working at a job for years and could never seem to get ahead. I was tired of struggling. I wanted more time, more money, and to create a legacy lifestyle that I could pass on to my children. I also needed an extra income stream to help my aging parents. Like you, I began searching for the right opportunity. I was looking for something where I didn't have to give up my full-time income from my job, but something I could do on the side.

What This Book Is Not

This book is NOT meant to be read as a result, but as a guide, or path for you to take the ambition that's been tugging at your heart and begin a journey to find the right opportunity to apply it. The contents of this book will not be telling you how to get-rich-quick. Success doesn't come without hard work and no one can guarantee your success. It's up to you!

This book is also NOT about being 'anti-jobs'. But you do need to understand we make money through a job, not from it. Someone can stop signing your paycheck at any time. It's happened to me, (several times) and maybe even to you. That's why I started creating multiple streams of income and I strongly believe everyone should consider doing the same thing.

I Was You

I wanted to write this book because I know there are lots of people who were like me. I followed the rules and began feeling stuck and frustrated by seeing other people living the life I wished I had. Even though I enjoyed what I did for a job, I couldn't see myself doing it for another 20 years. I didn't want to be like everybody else.

So, I began to search for opportunities and quickly became overwhelmed. There were so many so-called "experts" blasting me about how they made hundreds of thousands of dollars and how I could too. But everything seemed so complicated. I just wanted to pay off my debt, have money in the bank, and have several income streams coming in each month where we wouldn't have to be worried about retiring. In fact, one of my dreams was to retire early if I could. I knew what I didn't want. I didn't want to be in a business that was a passing fad or would require lots of time and investment. So, the years passed and every day I went to my job I had a restless ambition inside of me. I knew I was meant for something more. I believed that God wouldn't have given me all my dreams if there wasn't a way to achieve them.

INTRODUCTION

My wake-up call came the afternoon of March 24th. I was sitting by my wife's side in a small, unassuming hospital room. I was drained physically, and emotionally. I was getting ready to head down to the hospital's cafeteria when I was interrupted by a nurse saying we needed to get to the NICU NOW! You see, three days prior my wife had an emergency c-section and my son, 'RJ' was next door in the NICU. We were quickly shuffled into a private room with a widow looking into where our son was laying with a team of doctors surrounding him. One of the doctors was performing CPR on his little body.

As his Father I had to make the call. "Is he suffering?" I asked the nurse. The nurse replied with a heart-wrenching, "Yes, he is." "You have my permission to end CPR." We were then escorted back to our room where the realization of what just occurred drove us to a feeling I wish no parent must go through.

Within hours, a lady came into our room and announced we had to make some decisions. She said, "a couple of funeral homes provide cremations for free as a service for parents of babies who have passed away. Otherwise, here is a list of funeral homes and their estimated cost for their services." She dropped a large stack of papers on my wife's bed and left.

Even though my wife and I both worked, we were already struggling financially. We were recently married living in a 2-bedroom apartment and by no means living large. Every month was a struggle with the bills, and I was already feeling like I wasn't being the provider, and now father my new wife had expected me to be.

I'm embarrassed to say I decided to have the body of our son cremated, mainly because it was free. I knew right then and there I never wanted to be put in that situation again, where my life's decisions were made based not on how much we had, but on how much we didn't have.

I've started some small businesses in the past. They were successful for a short period of time, but dependent on me. All my money, all my time and all my risk. I read a couple of books by Robert Kiyosaki where he describes how the wealthy work to create passive, ongoing income. That's what I wanted! I had always been working for active, linear income. That's what we are all taught. I followed the rules like everyone else; I went to college, went to graduate school and began working as a professional only to be laid off three times, outplaced, and living paycheck to paycheck.

So, I started looking for opportunities. Through a friend of a friend I was introduced to a successful entrepreneur, Matt. Matt had spent most of his life as an entrepreneur. He had started a business on the side of a successful consulting business he had. Over a period of time he was making more money from his side-business than his full-time consulting business, so he had the opportunity to retire early and become a full-time husband, father, and now grandfather. He now travels, and does whatever he wants, whenever he wants; he owns his life. Over the past 15 years I have had the fortunate opportunity to have multiple multi-millionaires pour mentorship, leadership and wealth mentality into me.

I'm not saying that this book will be a magic bullet promising you the same thing. I listened and applied the teaching and mentorship I've received. Through this book I will outline what I learned to create successful businesses on the side of my career. I will provide you the path you can use to go through the same journey as I did, but in ¼ of the time as it took me.

Before you begin reading this book, I recommend you visit the book's website and take the short quiz, "Is Being a Sidepreneur Right for Me?" at www.sidepreneurbook.com. This will give you an insight to what being a Sidepreneur really entails and if you have what it takes. You will also find additional resources I've provided that will help you through-out the reading of this book.

PART ONE

{ *Sidepreneur:* side·pre·neur (sīd prən'ər)
noun: side+entrepreneur
    a person who operates a business on the
side of their full-time job. }

1. You Have A Restless Ambition

I was frustrated. Every year on my birthday I got depressed. Another year went by and I was nowhere closer to having a more successful and fulfilling life. I was stuck in an 'almost life'. I wasn't fulfilled or where I wanted to be.

I started dreaming big in high school. I created a long list of what I wanted. Yes, there was a big house, a Lamborghini, travel and money. But there were also the intangible things like being able to take care of my parents in their senior years, supporting ministries, and just having a peace of mind that my family will be taken care of if something should happen to me. I had big dreams, but the problem was that I didn't have a way to get them. I had a restless ambition.

I began looking for opportunities, probably like you. Fortunately, I found a niche opportunity through a friend of a friend which gave me the way to pay off my debts, have the ability to retire early, and have a passive, ongoing sideline income stream coming in month after month. From there, I took what I learned and created multiple streams of income that includes publishing books, speaking and helping those who are serious about making a change and leaving the land of average.

17

Whenever I begin to talk with someone that is looking for an opportunity, I like to ask them to place themselves on a quality of life scale. So, I'm going to start by asking you to do this now. Use the scale below and rank where you currently see yourself and your life where 10 is living the life of your dreams, and 1 is that your life stinks.

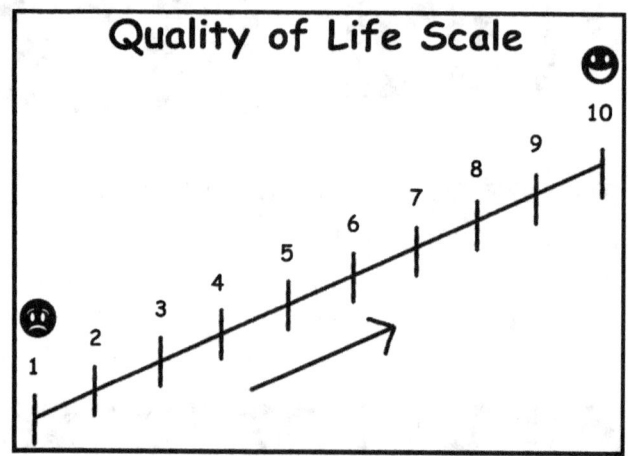

If you are like most people, you probably ranked yourself a 6 or 7. So, what is it you are missing that would raise you higher on the scale? Is it more time, more money, a peace of mind, the ability to travel more? What is it? It's important to know this. If you don't know what you are missing, how do you know what you should be working toward?

Where do you see yourself 5 years from now? NOT what do you want to be doing, but how do you see yourself living? It still surprises me the number of people who haven't stopped to think about this. If you don't know where you want to go, then how will you know how to get there or when you arrive? That's like calling me from your car on an Interstate and saying, "we're on the way!" "Terrific", I reply. "Where are you going?" "I don't know, but I'll know when we get there." How crazy it that conversation? That's exactly what you are doing when you begin a business without thinking about and writing down your vision of where you are going. I'll cover creating a vision in more detail in Part Three.

2. You Feel Like You Can Never Get Ahead

In 1997 I decided to go back to school and get a master's degree. I was still young and wanted to prove to myself that I could do it, but also give myself more knowledge to get into a long-term career. After 20 years and three layoffs later, I was still in the same place financially I had been before, working paycheck to paycheck, in debt, and struggling. Now, I had a house, more bills and a family depending on me.

Employees seek safe and secure jobs with good benefits. Sometimes employees get an annual raise, usually not higher than 5%. The problem with this is if you consider the annual cost of living adjustment (COLA) and the annual inflation rate, then you are lucky to break even. Our bills are going higher, our debt is going deeper, and our income is staying the same. That's why you are feeling like you are never getting ahead…because you're not! In fact, if you're not getting a 5% raise you may be going backwards.

So, what's the solution? Some people run out and get another part time job. I remember when I was living in an apartment I was told over and over that I was throwing my money away by not buying a house. Instead of paying money in rent, it could be going into the equity of my own house. That's how I look at getting a part time job.

As an employee, you are basically renting your life for the amount of money your employer is willing to pay you for that position. It's never the amount you're worth, but what the job is worth, and for as long as they decide they will pay it. It could end anytime they decide to end it. I know this first-hand because it's happened to me several times. Again, I'm not saying jobs are bad. You just need to understand it for what it is. It's a way to make a living. But, why not, while you have the benefit of an income from a job take some flexible unproductive time and turn it into an asset by creating something of your own.

> **"Insanity is doing the same thing over and over and expecting a different result."**
> —Albert Einstein

A Sidepreneur doesn't want to keep renting their life out, they want to OWN it. They want to start a business of their own where they can call the shots. Most people can't just quit what they're doing to venture out as an entrepreneur. I couldn't. So, I decided to keep doing what I was doing for my job and become an entrepreneur on the side; a Sidepreneur!

If you keep doing what you've been doing, you'll keep getting what you've been getting. Are you wanting to get ahead? You must **Do Something Different!** It's time to do something different!

3. You Want More Options

As I mentioned in the Forward, after my son, 'RJ' died I had a choice to make; pay for a funeral and burial or choose cremation that was provided as a free courtesy. I can't tell you that even if we had the disposable income to choose a burial that's what we would have done. But, because we didn't have the money, it narrowed our options in making our final decision.

The amount of money we make determines the options we have in our lives. When I first got a job, I was fine. But as the years passed, the cost of living increased, but my paycheck didn't. Yes, I did get small raises, but not enough to keep up with my expenses. I quickly found myself struggling and living paycheck to paycheck. This wasn't the way I imagined myself living, especially for the rest of my life. What happened to all of those hopes and dreams I had growing up?

Having more money doesn't make one evil. Money is just paper. It takes on the personality of the one that has it. Good people do good things with money, and bad people do bad things with money. But it takes money to live, eat, stay healthy and support causes. Having another income stream affords me the choice and quality of the automobile I drive, the quality of the neighborhood I live in, and the quality of where we go on trips.

Do you make your choices based on what you want, or how much it costs? A quick way to answer that question is by how you read menus. Do you read them from left to right based on what you want, or right to left based on the price?

> J—Just
> O—Over
> B—Broke

What are some options you would want from having multiple income streams? Taking care of your aging parents, helping a family member who is struggling, setting aside money for your children, or how about just being able to plan a vacation to where you want to go and not worrying about running out of money the rest of the month when you get back? Having a business on the side is not all about making more money, but the options money gives you.

4. You Want to Make a Difference

A Sidepreneur is someone who wants to not only make a difference in their life, but other people's lives. As I'm hitting my mid-life, I've began embracing the idea that this life is more and more about making a difference in the lives of others. It's disappointing that it's taken me this long, but at least I've recognized it and have put it into action. So, as I am living my life and building my business I have narrowed-in on the idea of making a positive difference in people's lives.

What's your passion? People have either given up or are working empty and unfulfilled. They don't have any purpose or passion in their lives. They've worked most of their lives without really accomplishing anything.

Too many people are living to get their value from other people, or, to just get a quick buck. Instead, I propose that we add value to others, not the other way around. My legacy won't be what I've acquired, but what I've left behind that lives on in and through other people. I have learned that if I live my life adding value to others and making a difference in their lives, the money will come. Many people look at making money backwards.

> **"You will get all you want in life if you help enough other people get what they want."**
> —Zig Ziglar

Taking our eyes off ourselves seems unnatural but is necessary if we want to make a difference. I know we need to address our motive as we strive to uplift and empower. I was told by my mentor that if I go out and add value to everyone, not just those who might be of benefit to me or would have a connection to my business, that it would come back in more ways than I could imagine. **I believe this!**

The more money I have, the more I can help those around me. I really like how Russel H. Conwell in his book *Acres of Diamonds* explains, "Money printed your Bible, money builds your churches, money sends your missionaries, and money pays your preachers, and you would not have many of them, either, if you did not pay them." There are many non-profit organizations that make a real difference and depend on donations and contributions. I, myself choose to support several organizations that mean a lot to what I believe in. One passion I have is finding people who are sincerely struggling and being able to anonymously pay off their medical bills, past due rent, car payment, etc. All of this takes MONEY! By becoming a Sidepreneur you can create a cashflow method that will fund what you are passionate about.

I firmly believe that as adults we are entrusted to return the favor in taking care of aging parents. I've seen first-hand how one fall can turn the household of an aged parent upside down. My parents who were able to live in their house and be independent quickly needed help. From one fall they now needed assist bars installed, a ramp installed, someone to clean their house and cook meals, and the list goes on. I'm fortunate that my parents had some money set aside for retirement and are not struggling. But I know they are in the minority and there are many seniors that don't have that ability.

5. You Want to Leave a Legacy

Who was your great, great, great grandfather? Do you know who he was or anything about him? What did he do and how did he live? I barely know anything about one of my grandfathers, much less my great, great, great grandfather. I know that my grandfather owned his own business, a pharmacy in Daytona Beach, FL. He and my grandmother didn't live lavishly, but saved money toward their retirement. They were able to enjoy their retirement years by traveling up and down the East Coast with an RV. I loved my grandparents. My grandfather passed away from Alzheimer's Disease in his 80's. My grandmother lived into her 90's. She didn't plan on living that long and outlived the money she and my grandfather had saved. The sad reality is that there are many today who are only in their 70's that have already outlived their money.

If either of your great, great, great grandparents created a legacy that lived on after their death, I would guarantee that you probably would know who they were and what they did. Foundations, memorials and trusts are built by people who leave a legacy. They are remembered.

I am a father to two girls. I am making a point of encouraging them to explore the opportunities to be a business owner. As parents we strive to give our children what we didn't have and keep them from making the same mistakes we made. One of my passions is to be able to create a strong passive, ongoing income that I can leave to not only my children, but grandchildren. I've met many children of business owners who, when I ask if they will be taking over the family business tell me that they either have no interest in the type of business their parents built, or after seeing the time and stress that their parents put into their business don't want to take on the same lifestyle.

Are you thinking past your lifetime? I believe most parents want to leave something of value to their kids, but don't have anything of value to pass on. Unfortunately, most parents only pass on debt. You see, if all you have is an income from a job, that income stops as soon as you stop working. I remember when a woman in a company I worked for died at an early age, in her 30's. Her position was posted within two days and her position was filled within two weeks.

As a Sidepreneur, you can take your unproductive time to create an income that can potentially live on after you die. I say potentially, because, as you will read later in Part Three, just by owning a business on the side of your job doesn't mean you will automatically be creating a passive, ongoing income. It comes down to the vehicle you choose as a Sidepreneur.

Create a life that will live on after you leave this Earth. Live a life that creates an influence.

A Sidepreneur...

Trades the good today for the great tomorrow!
Drives toward a vision of the future they want to create!
Chases knowledge!
Gets out of their comfort zone!
Is solution minded!
Accepts no excuses from themselves!
Competes against their best self!

PART TWO
Taking Control of Your Future

1. Lifestyle of the Rich and Famous

I've been entrepreneur-minded most of my life. I grew up in a middle-class family and saw my parents go to work five and six days a week for years. I am appreciative of what they provided and consider myself blessed. But I didn't want to live that life. I wanted to travel and live the life I saw on the *Lifestyles of the Rich and Famous*.

At the age of 25 I started my own business. It was an educational touring theatre company. I really had no idea what I was doing, but I had a dream of being a business owner and decided to jump in. It didn't take long until I was maxing out my credit card and investing fifty to sixty hours a week. I made it work and was successful for a while. But everything I was doing was trial and error and when it was an error, it was expensive. I was quickly in debt. But I was taking action.

In the past when I heard of a business owner that went bankrupt, I saw them as a bad businessperson and as a failure. I admit I couldn't have been more wrong! As I read and listened to successful people many were either much deeper in debt or had gone bankrupt in at least one of their businesses.

There's almost always a struggle-to-victory story behind the people we see in the "Rich and Famous." What they all have in common is patience, motivation, a big vision and perspective.

Did You Know...

Lady Gaga risked $3 million, all the money she had on a stage in hopes to catapult her career. It worked...

Will Smith—Before becoming The Fresh Prince of Bel-Air, Will had to sell practically everything he had to pay $2.8 million he owed to the IRS.

Walt Disney went broke and bankrupt over a film deal that went bad. He went on to create Mickey Mouse later and turned it into now, one of the world's largest companies.

Abraham Lincoln was in debt from the bad running of a store he once owned. Of course, he later went on to become President of the United States.

Larry King—Prior to his career in radio and film, Larry was in over $350,000 in debt.

Henry Ford—Before building his automobile empire, went bankrupt in 1903.

---

2. New Times...New Rules

I remember while growing up both my parents were in jobs not only for many years at the same place, but also somewhere that included some type of pension or retirement plan. They both went to college, got jobs and retired around sixty-five or soon after. I was told, as I'm sure you were, to get good grades in high school so I could go to college and get a degree that would help me go out and get a good job. Then, I could work until I'm 65, retire, buy an RV and enjoy my retirement days traveling like my grandparents. In the past, that's how it worked. People would stay in the same job at the same place for thirty to forty years.

This isn't how it is anymore! The rules that have worked in the past aren't working anymore and people aren't sure what to do about it. They are still trying to live by an old set of rules expecting things today to result in the way they did in the past.

I have interviewed hundreds of people who followed that advice and are sitting in student loan debt, working in a job that is nowhere associated to what they went to school for. According to *finder.com*, "28.28% of college graduates can't find a job in their field of study and 40.40% of people in the workforce are not even using their degree."[4]

I'm not insinuating that going to college is a bad idea. In fact, if you are planning to be a brain surgeon, PLEASE go to college. I went to college and have a master's degree. But, getting a degree doesn't guarantee that there's a job available for you in the field you studied. I know this first-hand because after working in my field of degree for four years, I haven't worked in it since. Over 20 years later, I'm still paying off thousands in student loan debt.

Today, employees rarely stay in the same position at the same place for more than five to ten years. In fact, you're more likely to see someone change jobs every two to four years. With the rise of technology, many companies have incorporated robotics, artificial intelligence, or are outsourcing jobs that were at one time being filled by local employees. It's a new time, and new times call for a change. I suggest everyone should invest their unproductive time now to create a "what-if" or Plan 'B' income. Become a Sidepreneur!

3. Is Your Way Working?

I'll never forget working for a very large company and, while walking through the company parking lot noticing that every car, for the most part, were similar makes and models. They all fell in the same price range. The only cars that were different, were those of the VP's and

---

4. www.finder.com/college-degree-value

WHO IS A SIDEPRENEUR?

upper management. The employees were one set of new tires away from being in a financial disaster.

How long have you been working in a job or career? Are you as far along as you thought you would be in savings, being out of debt, having more time and options? Have you been able to upgrade your lifestyle after working five, ten, twenty years at a job?

I have met dozens of people over 70 who are working in a restaurant or store. After getting to know them a little I found out they aren't working because they are bored, but because they HAD to get a part time job in their senior years just to make it. The money they got from their social security income wasn't enough. For some it was from a lack of planning, but for many it was because the money they thought would carry them through retirement was either lost through a stock market crash or didn't last as long as they predicted.

Again, I'm not anti-jobs. But it's time to take a real assessment of where you are and if what you're doing is getting you what you want long-term. A study by, *The Week* calls this, "The Age of Unretirement".[5] Life isn't a dress rehearsal and we are getting older every day. Don't fall into the trap of waking up at 60 realizing that you have little to no savings and getting the letter from the Department of Social Security only to learn that your social security check will only be one-third of what you are making now, if you're lucky. Of course, that's if social security is still around then.

4. Who's in Control?

I learned shortly after entering the workforce, the hard way, that if someone else signs your paycheck, they are in control of you financially. Shortly after earning my master's degree I landed a job in the north suburbs of Chicago. Everything was going great. I was getting high employee reviews and a raise every year. After working for four years I received a raise that was above the maximum amount employ-

---

5. www.theweek.com/articles/818253/age-unretirement

ees received after their reviews. You can imagine my excitement. Three months later… fifteen people were laid off, including me.

My eyes were opened after reading Robert Kiyosaki's book, *Cashflow Quadrant* learning that there are two types of income; active/linear income and ongoing, or passive income. Active, or linear income is renting your life for what the position is worth. It is based on your performance.

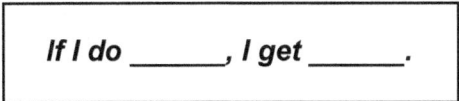

You are actively trading your hours for their dollars. It's called linear income because there will always be a ceiling to your income. The only way to increase what you are making through a linear income is either by making more money, i.e. getting a raise, or working more hours. You will never be in control. Even if you are self-employed, there is still a ceiling on your income because there are only 24 hours in a day.

Ongoing, passive income is just as it sounds, but with a larger business ownership thought in mind. It is doing the work once, and continually getting paid for the work you did.

> **If I do _____, I build _____.**

Your income isn't in bondage to a dollar amount per hour of how many hours you work. The ceiling is lifted, and you are in control of how much you make. With ongoing income, you are doing a type of work one time, but continue to get paid for that work for months or years later. In some cases, you will continue to get paid even after you die. Of course, you won't be spending any of it, it will go to your estate.

5. The Mindset of a Sidepreneur

After my first experience of being laid-off I returned home to North Carolina where I began creating multiple streams of income. I was working full time but began teaching for a couple of colleges on the side. But my income was still unstable. I was making more money, but it was still a linear income. Every semester my pay was determined whether my classes had enough students to run. Many times, my classes were cancelled for low enrollment and I had no control over it.

My first taste of creating an ongoing income was when I wrote and published a book. I am one of those creative, ambitious types who saw others around me publishing books, so I wanted to prove to myself that I could do it also. Did I know how to? Nope! It was a lot of trial and error. But, I did it anyway. It was my first attempt at publishing and, even though I didn't do it for the money, I began to get royalties every month and for the first time stepped into the life of creating a passive, ongoing income as a Sidepreneur. I was hooked.

I began asking myself why it took me so long to figure this out and why other people aren't more excited about doing the same thing. As I met and talked with other people in the marketplace, I could see the emptiness in their eyes. Had they become complacent? Did they try and then give up? Have they been stuck in the land of mediocracy so long they that they have accepted it as their fate or the thought of doing something different made them too uncomfortable? Or maybe people didn't truly believe there was a way to achieve their dreams and lost their hope? Whatever the reason, I knew there were more people in the world like me and I made the decision to help them break out of the masses to create a legacy lifestyle.

A Sidepreneur is someone who wants to make a life while making a living. They work hard at their jobs and are loyal employees but have a restless spirit of ambition that tells them they can be more, have more and do more. They want to break free from average and strive to have a purpose and live a life of fulfillment.

When someone decides to become a Sidepreneur they understand that creating a business on the side doesn't come without hard work, time, and the development of oneself. In addition, there is some risk involved. Sometimes there's more risk of lowering your ego, changing, getting out of your comfort zone and ridding oneself of negativity, bad habits or wrong associations than there is of a financial risk.

6. It's Time to do Something Different!

After being laid off from my second job I realized what I was doing wasn't working and it was time to do something different. Having a job for an income was a good thing to have. It paid the bills, but I couldn't depend on it. I needed more money to pay for my student loans and the debt that I built while looking for another job. There had to be a better way to make more money than running out and getting another part-time job. That is what I saw everyone else doing. If the majority was correct in the way they made money, everybody would be rich.

Soon after I published my book, I knew I wanted to create an ongoing income stream, so I began to search for the right opportunity. I knew being an investor or getting into real estate would create an ongoing income stream, but I didn't have the money (or patience). I certainly didn't have the investment to start my own franchise and I knew if I bought into a franchise, I wouldn't have a job, but would then own a job.

Shortly after I began my search, I was introduced to the network marketing industry. I didn't know much about it at the time, but the more I learned I began to see a way to create the ongoing income stream I wanted using this model. Many successful people like Les Brown, Robert Kiyosaki, Sir Richard Branson, Paul Zane Pilzer and Warren Buffett invested in or endorsed this type of business model.[6] I figured if these people who were a lot more successful than I was supported this type of business model, I should be opened minded to it as well.

---

6. www.businessforhome.org/2014/09/hall-of-fame-mlm-celebrities/

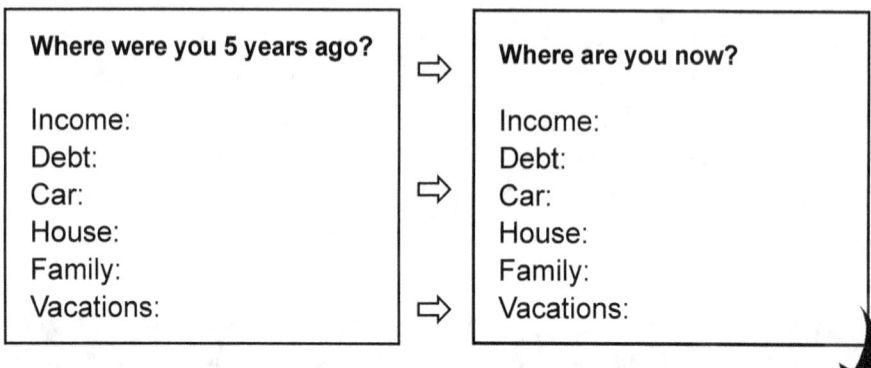

Where were you 5 years ago?	Where are you now?
Income:	Income:
Debt:	Debt:
Car:	Car:
House:	House:
Family:	Family:
Vacations:	Vacations:

Where will you be 5 years from now if you don't change anything?

I did my due diligence in researching the legality and business model presented to me and decided that it was the right fit for me. I know everyone has their own opinions about network marketing and many are either opposed to it or may have had a previous experience that was negative. Regardless, it was the path I chose.

If you are looking at me now, I am continuing to add vehicles that produce additional streams of income such as speaking engagements, a membership site, another book and creating online courses. The first step is to make the decision to start to do something different. The second step is to not quit.

7. Walking Through the Minefield

In several of John C. Maxwell's books he stresses the importance of mentorship. I've already experienced several attempts at trial and error and realized that if I'm going to be walking through a minefield, it would be wise to be the second person following in the footsteps of a leader who's been through that minefield before. It hurts less that way. Sidepreneurs value mentorship.

Having a mentor will not only save you a lot of time, but also a lot of money. It will keep you from making the same mistakes others have made… that's if you listen and accept their mentorship. One important lesson I learned early-on was if I already knew what it took to be financially independent, I would already be financially independent.

A friend of a friend introduced me to my coach and mentor. He was once like me, working long hours and working paycheck to paycheck. He owned his own consulting business but had little to no time for his family and knew something needed to change. He grabbed ahold of an opportunity, became a Sidepreneur, and now is a successful entrepreneur living the lifestyle I wanted; early retirement, traveling with his family, and is financially independent. My mentor not only agreed to mentor me, but also introduced me to many other mentors who were more successful than he was. They all started in the same place as me, as a Sidepreneur starting businesses while still working a job. If they could do it, so could I.

As you are beginning your path to be a Sidepreneur, I can't stress enough the importance in finding someone who has done what it is you are wanting to do. Even if you are venturing into a niche that is brand new and uncharted, there are people who have done something similar to what it is you are wanting to do. You may need to invest some money into getting access to their business system or knowledge, but it can be well worth it. Of course, be sure to do your due diligence prior to jumping into and paying for someone's program. I'll cover more on what to look for in a mentor and where to find a good coach and mentor in Part Six.

PART THREE The Sidepreneur Ingredients

1. A Big Vision ... Design the Life You Want to Create

Where are you going? What's your purpose in life? Do you know…? Do you have a vision of where it is you want to go? Is what you are doing now getting you the lifestyle you want? If you don't know what you want long term, you'll make poor short-term decisions. If you don't know where you are going, how will you know when you get there? Decide what you want first, then figure out how to get there.

If you don't have a vision of where it is you are going, then you'll live a life going from problem to problem and your life will be a wandering generality. I know that sounds harsh, but it's true. Your vision can, and should include multiple areas in your life; finances, family, spirituality, career, awards or levels of achievement, etc.

> ### 5 Steps to Creating Your Vision

Step 1. Begin—Create Your Vision

It's sad, but most people meander through life without a vision. They live a life of mediocrity, living day to day with no real purpose. You can always change or adjust your vision as you grow. Create a vision for your life. "Your life" includes all the goals that you want to reach. This can include the size house you want to live in, where you want to be in your business, the vision for your kids and family, attaining certain awards or recognition, etc.

Step 2. Write Your Vision Down

According to research, less than 3% of Americans have their goals written down. Many people have thought about them, but that's not good enough. When it comes to writing your vision, the secret is for them to be "hand-written". Now, I'm like everyone else who says, "Yea but Rik, it's quicker for me to type it in a note on my phone plus I can whip out my phone anytime I need to be reminded of it." There's magic in handwriting your vision. Personally, I hand-write my vision and then take a photo of it using my phone.

Tips to writing your vision:
- *Be specific*
- *Be realistic*
- *Put a date on it*
- *Write down goals*
- *Review it daily*

Step 3. Set Your Vision High

Some people set their vision too high. I'm all about reaching, but you need to be realistic or you will feel defeated quickly. Others do the opposite and set their vision too low. Find the balance.

Your vision should be high enough where it gives you a challenge and is set over the distractions that will come against you. Distractions will come. Expect it! Why do a lot of people never reach their vision? Their vision is too low, and they let distractions knock them off course.

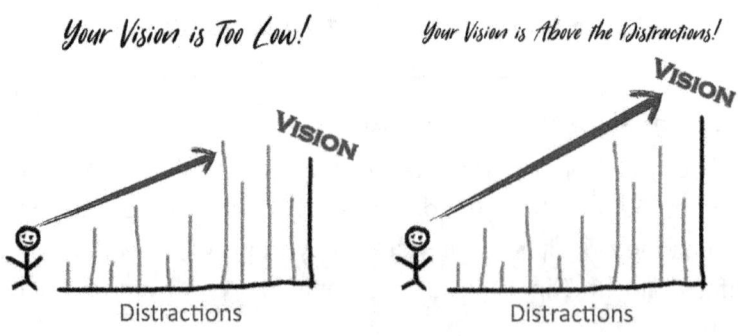

Your Vision is Too Low!   Your Vision is Above the Distractions!

Distractions   Distractions

Step 4. Keep Your Vision in Front of You

You've made it this far, but if you don't review and read your vision daily, the distractions of life will cause your vision to be a hopeful wish of the past. The more you read your vision (out loud) the more your mind will accept it to be true.

A great tool that a lot of people create is a Vision Board. There are many ways to do this, but the idea is to find photos that relate to your vision and post them on a board that you see daily to remind you (and your brain) of your vision. The photos will be a daily visual reminder of your vision.

To find a how-to on creating a Vision Board,
visit **www.sidepreneurbook.com/resources**.

Step 5. Move Toward Your Vision

Set some daily actionable goals that will move you toward your vision. A lot of people spend their time looking backwards. Do you drive looking in the rear-view mirror instead of the front windshield? You can learn from the past, but you can't change it. If you don't have a daily plan of moving toward your goals that will help you reach your vision, then you will remain in your daily habits that got you to where you are today. Remember, if you keep doing the same things you've been doing, you'll keep getting the same results you've been getting.

Every successful company has a vision statement. Some people may call it a mission statement. Why not you? What are you living and working toward? Do you want to live a life of purpose? Then having a vision for your life is the place to start. But you need to start now. Your life right now is as simple as it's ever going to be. Think bigger than what you can see. When I was writing out my vision, I didn't have a guide sheet or template to follow. So, I made my own! To help you define and write your vision I've included the worksheet I made at www.sidepreneurbook. com/resources.

2. A Vehicle

If you wanted to go from North Carolina to California what vehicle would you use to take you there? There are several factors that will determine which one you might choose. For those into aerobic fitness, you may choose a dependable bicycle. If you had plenty of time and wanted to take in the scenic stops along the way while being efficient, you would choose an economical car. If you decided you wanted to be adventurous and take the off-road routes, you would choose a 4-wheel drive vehicle. An exotic car would get you there quickly and in style. But, if you needed to get there tomorrow, you would take an airplane.

Any vehicle will take you from North Carolina to California. You need to know which vehicle is right for you, where you want to go and how quickly you want to get there. I wanted early retirement, financial freedom and a peace of mind and I quickly learned that a job was the wrong vehicle to get me where I wanted to go. I needed another vehicle. As I searched for side-line opportunities, I discovered hundreds, if not thousands, of vehicles. First, I had to decide where I wanted to go and then how quickly I wanted to get there. I designed my own Vision Worksheet and realized that the vehicle I needed was one that was dependable and would outlast me by creating a passive, ongoing income.

It's important to understand that there are two ways to create income; linear and ongoing. As I mentioned earlier in the book, a job and being self-employed creates an active/ linear income. You are trading hours for dollars. It's based on your effort. Even being a full-time business owner is creating an active/linear income. If you decide to become a full-time business owner and become your own boss, you have more freedom, but the trade is that you usually now have less time. Now instead of having a job, you *own* the job.

Choosing the right vehicle for where you want to go is an important decision a Sidepreneur should make before beginning. Take the time to first know where you want to go, how quickly you want to get there, then find the vehicle that works for you. Remember that you can always have multiple vehicles, and that's a great goal to work toward. But start with one then add as you go along.

3. Knowledge

Warren Buffet once said, "The best investment you can make is the investment in yourself." If you want to make a lifestyle change, you will have to make a change in the way you think. A lot of people stop reading and learning as soon as they leave school. If you believe you are going to improve your life and not improve yourself, you're wrong. If you already knew what it took to become financially independent, you would already be financially independent, and you wouldn't be reading this book. Chase knowledge from those that have it. When you change the way you think, you will change your life. Find a mentor!

I learned a long time ago that I can either learn from my mistakes, or somebody else's. It was less expensive for me to learn from somebody else's mistakes. Regardless of the direction you want to take as a Sidepreneur, the odds are that someone else has tried it, or done it.

Unfortunately, I have met many people who sought mentorship from the wrong person. Parents, friends or co-workers can be an unending source of unqualified advice. But, if they haven't been successful in what they are giving you advice on, why are you listening to them? That's like me asking for marriage advice from someone who has been divorced three times. Seek knowledge from someone who has done what it is you are wanting to do and has a vested interest in your success.

4. Skills

Over the years I've developed many skills. Some I chose to learn and develop, and others I was forced to. Regardless how I came about the skill, in the long run I don't regret any of them. In fact, I love learning new things. From graphic design to video production and effects, starting a business of my own to developing people skills and a network, and moving from a brick and mortar business to online businesses and opportunities, I've morphed and acquired new skills to keep up with technology and where the opportunities are now found.

If you like to stay the same and not improve yourself and your skills, being a Sidepreneur is NOT for you. But it you are willing to grow, change and develop new skills, then the doors to new opportunities will swing wide. Success is not a destination, but a journey. Learning new skills are part of that journey, and now with everything that's available on the Internet, there is no excuse not to learn what you need to learn to make up the gaps in the skills you need for the opportunities you are searching for.

Writing a book is a great example. I wrote my first book in 2014. I knew nothing about self-publishing, designing a book cover, style, distribution, etc. But that didn't stop me. I did it anyway and learned as I went.

The good news is that you don't have to learn on your own. When I started my online-based retail business I was stretched to learn people skills, sales, networking, teamwork and goal setting. Fortunately, I was able to plug into a mentor who helped me in developing these skills. I was able to shadow him, follow his example and have access to an education system. This cut my learning curve drastically. Therefore, it is to your advantage to find someone that's done what it is you are wanting to do and follow their system and what they've done. When you search online, you'll find that there's no shortage of educational systems. Do yourself a favor and do your due diligence before choosing someone's system. There are many imposters trying to sell their "proven" system when in fact, it's only someone trying to make a quick buck.

Expect to invest some money when you choose to use someone's system and gain access to their knowledge and experience. It's only fair since they already put the time, trial and error and materials for you to use and follow. Be warry of those promising to get-rich-quick. A good education/ business system can save you lots of time, energy and wasted money and will be well worth it in the end if it's a proven, successful educational system.

5. Persistence

Setbacks, distractions and negative people are all to be expected. There will be days when you feel not just tired or frustrated, but you feel like throwing in the towel and quitting. It happens to everyone who is stepping out of the land of mediocrity and doing something different. It's just like when you learned to ride a bike. I haven't heard of many people that just jumped on a bike for the first time and started riding it down the street. I remember falling many times, getting scrapes, bruises, running into trees and being frustrated. Every time I felt like giving up, I saw how other kids were riding their bikes and I knew if they could do it, so could I.

Whatever opportunity you decide to pursue on the side, there are probably others who went down the same path, had similar challenges, but persisted and became successful. Having a clear vision of what you are working toward and where you are going will keep you moving forward when times get tough. Celebrate small successes and milestones.

When I was developing my people skills and learning to network it wasn't comfortable. I didn't like talking to other people because I had a low self-image. There were many times when I felt like it wasn't worth it, and I wanted to give up. Before I entered business, I was a professional actor for 15 years. Onstage, I had no problem singing and speaking in front of thousands of people. Offstage, I was a different person. I kept to myself. Being an actor was just a cover for my low self-image.

What turned me around was learning that networking is a skill, and skills can be learned. I was persistent in developing my self-image and confidence through reading and positive association. Now, I consider networking as one of my top assets. I'm glad I didn't quit.

6. Patience

I will admit that the characteristic of patience has alluded me most of my life. I've never been good at having patience. A few years after our son, 'RJ' was born, I was blessed to be the father to a girl, and years later another daughter when we made the decision to adopt. As my daughters are entering their pre-teens, I can say that my patience has been challenged like never before.

It's important when you begin the path to creating a side business that you think long term. As I mentioned before, we are not talking about getting rich quick. So, as you are working toward a 3-5 year vision, having the patience to take your business one day at a time is essential. Just as it takes a part-time student attending college longer to achieve their degree compared to a student going full-time, as a Sidepreneur you are working part-time hours, so getting things up and running may take you a little longer. Give yourself, as well as your side-business, time to grow.

7. Thick Skin

As mentioned earlier, when you rise out of the crowd of average, you will have tomatoes thrown at you. If you are not, then you are not rising high enough. I had a habit of analyzing what others were saying about me and worried what other people thought about what I was doing. It caused me a lot of unnecessary anxiety and stress.

My mentor once asked me, "do those people pay your bills?", "will they take care of your wife and children if something happens to you?" He continued, "then why are you worried what anyone says about you?" That's when I decided to have a thick skin and not take to heart any of what the nay-sayers said about me or what I was doing.

Decide that you will have a thick skin. People who criticize others who are stepping out have either lost their dream, feel intimidated, or simply like being a negative person. Look back in history to anyone that's done anything that's made a difference. I guarantee they had people throwing tomatoes at them. Take those tomatoes and make a salad; or ketchup, whichever you prefer.

8. Self -Motivation

Over the years I've attended 75+ conferences for entrepreneurs. With the exception of one, they were all fantastic. I left with a new mindset, a renewed energy and the motivation to conquer any odds because success is right around the corner. A week later, I felt beat-down, tired and sometimes frustrated. The motivation I received, as valuable as it was, was external. The speakers were inspirational, the atmosphere was positive, and the information was invaluable. But the motivation was temporary.

Self-motivation is internal. Let's face it, sometimes after working at a job all day you may not feel like putting any time into your side-business. Having self-motivation and a vision gives you the push you need to break any external factors that are trying to hold you back and keep you from moving toward your goals and vision.

---

5 Things to Help Your Self-Motivation

1. Keep a strong vision in front of you
2. Make a daily commitment toward your vision
3. Have daily work habits
4. Proper time management
5. Develop a growth mindset through listening to positive, inspirational audios, reading self-development books and having positive association

---

PART FOUR

L et's get honest here, not everyone is cut out, or will decide to be a Sidepreneur. This isn't about winning the lottery on the side of your job. It's about starting a business on the side of your job. Having a business on the side of your job will take time, effort, work and patience. It's not get-rich-quick. But I found that it can be very rewarding. I like to view it as 'the shortcut'. Yes, it may take 3-5 years to create a profitable business on the side, but what's the alternative? Work 40 to 45 years and retire making maybe 1/3 of the income you're making now? Having a side business is a shortcut to what everybody else is doing. So, if you want to have what other people don't have, you must do what other people are not willing to do.

1. Get out of your Comfort Zone

Let's face it. When you become a Sidepreneur you are already, by default doing something different. You are venturing outside of the comfort zone of "average". Remember that many others have gone before you. You are not and will not be the only one that has ventured outside of their comfort zone.

Success is found on the other side of your comfort zone. You may need to do things you haven't done before or develop some skills you've never used like making sales, developing a network of people, making videos or creating online content. When you get out of your comfort zone you will have doubters, haters, obstacles and you will make mistakes.

2. Develop Belief

Success rises and falls in proportion to the belief you have. The greater your belief, the greater your success. If you think you can, or don't think you can... either way you're right. Belief is sometimes difficult to keep up if you've had past failures or have been struggling toward a goal for a long time. That's when having patience and a vision can lift you up and carry you forward.

---

5 Steps to Increase Your Belief

---

1. Know that you are better than you think you are

Most people sell themselves short. They see themselves as they are, not where they can be. Or, they fall into the trap of comparing themselves to other people; their weaknesses to other people's strengths. I encourage you to sit down and take a strength analysis. You have more to offer than you think. Tell yourself, "I'm just as good as the other person" not "They are better than me." Say, "I have what it takes" not "I'm not good enough."

2. Think positively, not negatively

Take control of your thoughts and words. When an opportunity comes your way tell yourself, "This is my opportunity, my moment" not "I can't." You need to condition your mind to thinking and speaking positive and success. We have negativity and failure attitudes all around us. That's the way average people think. You're not average. Recognize the inner voice of failure and kick it out.

3. Think bigger!

Have big dreams and goals. Understand that being successful at anything takes time and patience. Put your big vision in front of you. This is where using a Vision Board comes in handy. See yourself as a successful Sidepreneur. Don't look at how things are now, but as they will be.

4. Know you can do it

Odds are that others have done what it is you are wanting to do and if they have done it, so can you. Once you believe that you can do something, your mind goes to work to figure out ways to go and do it. What you do depends largely on what you believe you can do. If you believe you can do something, the how to do it will naturally come.

5. Surround yourself with other believers

To increase your belief, hang around other people who will support you and encourage you and your dreams and ambitions. It's a fact that your attitude, personality, thinking and success is determined and formed by the people you hang around with and by your environment.

Think about everyone who has made a discovery, created an invention or developed an empire. All those people have one thing in common, they all believed what they wanted to do could be done. I can say that I've had many, many ideas for movies, inventions and businesses, but never followed through on them because I didn't believe they would be successful. Truth be told, I didn't have belief in myself. Before you launch out to strike it rich in a new side-venture, you need to first discover the gold that's inside you.

3. Get the Right Thought Process

If you change the way you are going to create an income, you will also need to change the way you think. You are the product of your thoughts. As mentioned earlier, if I already knew how to be financially independent, I would be financially independent. Everyone wants to be more, do more and have more. What differentiates the doers from the don't doers are their thoughts. You must review not only how you think, but what you think about.

I challenge you to take an inventory of what you think about for a full day. Are you thinking, "I can do this!" or "I'll give it a try"? Or, "I believe I can be successful at anything I set my mind to!" or are you saying, "I've failed at pretty much everything else, I'll probably fail at this too"?

Why don't more people have a better thought process? Sometimes we think we already have one, we don't want to change, or we don't want to make the conscious effort. It takes effort to change your thought process and a lot of times it's not fun. We learn a lot about ourselves in the process as well as the areas where we need to change. Ask yourself, "what can I do to be a better person today?". Plan to develop and improve your thoughts daily.

> ## Steps to Getting the Right Thought Process

1. Cut out the Negative!
Are you the type of person that sits and watches TV for hours, worse yet, the news? I made the decision long ago to be the gatekeeper to my mind and cut out watching mindless hours of TV. What music are you listening to? There have been many times I've stopped at a traffic light and had to roll up my window to protect my children from hearing the "music" littered with profanity from a car next to me. Instead of listening to the radio, listen to something positive.

2. Put positive in your mind!
Listen to positive audios or watch inspiring videos. Hang around people who will speak positive into you and encourage you. You've had years of negative placed into your mind. It won't just leave, and you can't delete it. What you can do is saturate the negative with positive.

3. Speak positive to yourself!
A lot of times we are our own worst enemy. We tear ourselves down with our own words and thoughts we speak to ourselves. Your subconscious mind hears everything you tell it and believes it as true. Every time you speak, your subconscious mind is hearing you and program-

ming itself. There is proven science behind how what you say to yourself builds you up or tears you down. (For more information about your words and on your subconscious mind, visit www.sidepreneurbook. com/resources/books.)

4. Create the Right Attitude

Your attitudes are a matter of choice. Average people let circumstances determine their attitude. Your attitude determines how you act, and how you act will determine what you attract. So, before anything will change on the outside, you must first change on the inside.

No one wants to be around someone with a sour attitude. You know those types of people, where everything is gloomy, and the world is out to get them. Nothing good ever happens to them and as they sang on Hee Haw, "if it weren't for bad luck, I'd have no luck at all." People with poor attitudes repel others. The only thing they attract are other negative minded people who will join them wallowing in their mind-mud. The good news is that you can decide to change your attitude anytime you wish.

Decide to have PMA, Positive Mental Attitude every day. It will take work and a conscience effort. Be prepared to slip every now and then, but the more you work on having the right attitude and view of other people, life and opportunities, the more it will turn into a habit. Pretty soon, you'll be able to quickly recognize when your attitude is slipping and when others don't have a PMA.

Have you noticed that you slowly take on the mannerisms and speech of those you hang around with? At every job I was in I was challenged because I constantly heard co-workers complaining, whining and gossiping. They were miserable and wanted everyone else to know it and console their unhappiness. They felt stuck in a rut and everything was negative, negative, negative.

Years ago, before I knew the importance of having the right attitude, I was working for the owner of a company who enjoyed talking down to people, spoke to others in a rude way, and treated people like they were insignificant. Within a short time of being around him, I found myself doing the same thing. My wife and those close to me noticed. I was becoming a product of that environment. It wasn't until I left there that I realized how far my attitude had slipped. I had literally become a different person; one I didn't like.

Just as you will take on the bad attitudes of others, listening and hanging around others with a PMA will rub off on you as well. Your environment does make a difference and you get to create your own environment. You may be limited while you are at your job as to who is around you, but you do choose if you are going to participate in the company gossip, complaining and negative conversations.

The same ingredients you use to keep the right thought process will also improve your thought process. When you have a **P**ositive **M**ental **A**ttitude, you become a **P**erson **M**oving **A**head. Every day when you wake up you get to choose the attitude you will have for that day. Don't be the person that wakes up on the "wrong side of bed". Choose each day to always get up on the right side of the bed and make every day a great day.

5. Create the Right Atmosphere

My mother told be over and over that I am who I hang around with. She was right! You are the product of your environment. Just as flowers will bloom and grow in the right atmosphere, sun, fertile ground and rain, as a successful Sidepreneur you need to live in an environment where you have support and can grow.

> **What Can You Do to Create the Right Atmosphere?**

1. Get around people who are more successful than you.

We tend to want to hang around others where we are comfortable and not challenged. If you want to grow, find an atmosphere where you are not the brightest or most successful. You will be forced to stretch and develop your thoughts, habits and knowledge.

2. Hang around other dreamers.

There are other people who are like you and are also stepping out and wanting to improve their lives. Find a group of people who are going somewhere and are forward focused. They can keep you encouraged and motivated. If you had a campfire full of coals and took one out, what would happen? It's a silly question, it would cool off. But what happens when you put it back around the other hot coals? Its fire stays lit. Find other dreamers and get around them; people who will keep your coal hot.

3. Get in a positive environment.

Here in North Carolina where I live, we have fields of Kudzu. It's a creeping vine that chokes out other plants as it spreads over the ground. It seems to be everywhere. You won't see any flowers in a Kudzu field because everything besides the trees have been choked out and died. The same goes with who you are hanging around with. If they are negative or happy swimming in the pool of mediocracy, that's not the right atmosphere for you. They will choke out your ambition and dreams. Find others who are positive and encouraging. Weed out the Kudzu in your life.

4. Be allowed to take risks.

A good atmosphere includes being in a place where you can take risks and where failure is not seen as your enemy. Failure is not bad, it's a stepping-stone to success. We all make mistakes. Every successful person has failed at something, but they learned from it and moved forward.

5. Grow yourself.

Sadly, most people don't value continual learning and personal growth. Find an atmosphere where personal growth is encouraged. It's not very expensive and it's an investment in yourself. You'll also be helping other people toward their success and dreams.

6. Make a Plan

When I decided to attend graduate school, I was assigned a graduate advisor who worked with me in laying out the schedule I needed to have for the next two years. He took on the role of a mentor through my graduate program. I'm grateful that I listened to him. I didn't realize it, but some of the classes I needed to take were only offered once every two years, so if I didn't plan ahead to register for them when they were available, I would have to wait for another couple of years to be able to take them. My advisor saw a bigger picture than I did because he had a different vantage point and was invaluable in helping me plan out my time as a graduate student.

Very few people have sat down to map out their plan for their lives. I would venture to say that the farthest most people have gotten to mapping a plan for their lives was meeting with a career advisor their senior year in high school. Sadly, that's not really a plan, but a guess. How does a high school senior know what they want to do for the rest of their lives? There are those few who knew in high school that they wanted to be a physician, attorney, engineer, etc. But I've asked many college students what their long-term ambitions are and 8 out of 10 have no clue.

If you are going to take your time outside of your job to invest toward an entrepreneurial endeavor, you need a plan. Start with the result you are wanting, then work backwards. There are many people who have given up on their dreams and ambitions because they don't break-down their long-term vision into bite-size, monthly and daily activities. If you don't take your plan and break it down to simple activities, you will quickly feel overwhelmed and quit.

When I was in college, I was required to jog for a physical education class I took. Truth be told, I didn't realize that this was going to be a requirement for the class, or I probably wouldn't have taken it. Prior to that, the only time I ran was when a buffet opened, and I wanted to be first in line. The instructor didn't tell me to go out and run three miles. I first ran ¼ mile, then a week later ½ mile, and so on until I worked up to three miles. I broke the big goal down to weekly, smaller goals.

Every business owner makes a business plan before they launch a business. You're an entrepreneur. Make a plan. Find a mentor that will help and guide you and then follow the plan they used. It will save you time, money and lots of stress. Remember to include time for family, your faith, and time by yourself to just stop and think. I've included a worksheet that can help you in making a plan at www.sidepreneurbook. com/resources.

Inch by inch, success is a cinch.

To find a how-to on making a time plan,
visit **www.sidepreneurbook.com/resources**.

7. Take Action

When I decided to take a break from being a professional actor I returned to my hometown and made the decision to start my own educational touring theatre company. I knew nothing about how to do it. I had to learn everything on my own. I'm going to date myself by telling you that the Internet wasn't born yet. I remember finding (through a phone book) and going to the N.C. Dept. of Revenue to research what licenses I needed, what I needed to do to hire employees, report my earning etc. I then headed to the local IRS office to do the same thing. To complicate matters, I decided, to save money to do bulk mailings for marketing. Have you ever seen the requirements the post office has for one to make bulk mailings? I'm surprised I didn't quit right then.

But after weeks of going from office to office it came time to jump in and do something. My prime target market were elementary schools, so if I wanted to make money I had to launch while schools were meeting. If I procrastinated, I would have lost my window of opportunity and prolong the time it took me to start my business. Did I make mistakes? Of course! But I learned from them, adjusted and moved forward. I took action.

If all you do is read this book, get inspired, but don't act, then don't expect to get anything in return. Nothing happens until something happens. You must get up to go up. Yes, planning, researching and doing your due diligence is important, but there comes a time to jump in and do something.

> ### The 5 Action Stealers:
>
> 1. Fear
> 2. Doubt
> 3. Distractions
> 4. Procrastination
> 5. Laziness

PART FIVE

Five Obstacles to Being a Sidepreneur

1. The Three Fears

Fear is an enemy to success. It has stopped would-be bestselling authors from writing, life changing doctors from going to medical school and world changing entrepreneurs from starting a business. I strongly believe that almost everyone who has lived has had ideas within them that, if acted upon would had changed not only their lives, but the lives of millions of others.

As I mentioned I was a professional actor for over 15 years and never had the fear of speaking or performing in front of others. In fact, I jump at every chance I get to do so. For years I didn't understand anyone who was afraid of getting up in front of a classroom of peers to simply say their name. Later I learned that to them, the fear is real.

As one starts down the path of creating a business on the side of their jobs they will eventually face one of three fears; the fear of what other people will think, the fear of failure, the fear of success, or a combination of two or more. To know how to overcome the fear, you first need to identify your fear and what you are battling against.

Fear One: *What Other People Think*

"What if they think ...?", "What if I...?" Sound familiar? I believe that **Fear** is what stops most people from becoming successful, primarily the fear of what other people think (or what you *THINK* they are thinking.) Success is built around networking and speaking to other people. When people are afraid of what others are thinking about them, this keeps them from really branching out, meeting new people, and networking toward success.

I guess, because I started acting at a young age, the fear of speaking in front of others never developed. In my professional and business life, I have used this to my advantage when I network. Now, I'm not saying I am a people person. I didn't go out of my way to speak to someone unless I had a reason. I'd rather keep to myself. Networking is a lot different than being on a stage. Onstage you have bright lights shining in your eyes where you usually can't see the audience. When speaking to another person they are right there, standing in front of you.

As most people do, I have run into that little voice asking, "Will they think I am weird for starting a conversation?" or "What if I say something wrong?". It wasn't until my business mentor pointed out that if I am thinking these things, then I am thinking selfishly. How many of these little conversations in my head have the word, "I" or "me" in them? He was right. Whenever one has fear thoughts, most of the time it is all about them, not who they are talking to.

> **"Most people do not listen with the intent to understand; they listen with the intent to reply."**
> Stephen R. Covey

So, one of the ways to overcome this fear is to take our eyes off ourselves and put them on the other person. In fact, that's what actors are required to do on the stage, listen to the other character and then respond.

Here are 5 exercises I've applied that may help you to quiet the fear of what other people may be thinking and what may be holding your success back:

1. *Take a genuine interest in meeting new people.*

2. *Listen to want to learn something new about the other person you are speaking to.*

3. *Take a class in improvisation. This will teach you great listening skills.*

4. *Find a way that you can help them, not the other way around.*

5. *Provide an uplifting and encouraging word to the people you talk to.*

Fear Two: *The Fear of Failure*

Understand that success is built on failure. Most people never succeed because they never start. The possibility of failure defeats them in their mind at the birth of opportunity. Fear has kept many would-be successful people in bondage through the abortion of opportunities. Entrepreneurs convert their fear into excitement and the drive of a challenge. Action cures fear. Know that there really is no failure when you learn from every experience. It's only when you quit or give-up that it becomes failure.

> **"Most great people have attained their greatest success just one step beyond their greatest failure."**
> —Napoleon Hill

Fear Three: *The Fear of Success*

Yes, you can have a fear of success. It's happened to me. I've asked questions such as, "if I create a membership website and have thousands of members, will I be able to provide quality content that will keep them coming to my site for information?" or "when I have a network of hundreds of people depending on me as a mentor and leader, will I be able to provide them the knowledge and leadership they need to reach their dreams and goals?" "What if I let them down?"

Having a fear of success has held the same amount of people from taking action as the fear of failure. Having a network of mentors to lean on and reach up to is one way to overcome this fear. If you are trying to go it alone, you can find yourself in trouble. But, when you realize it's not all on your shoulders and only dependent on you, then you have the effort of a team. Study every successful person and you will see that they have a team behind them.

2. Insecurity

So many people want to **be** different, **do** different, and **have** different. We are surrounded by opportunities. Over the years, I have spoken to and even interviewed hundreds of people who *SAY* they are looking for opportunities for more money, leadership, and a better way of living. But, out of all those people, only a small handful have followed through.

Why did so many people not follow through? Were they lying to me, or themselves? They chose to stay in a life of mediocrity. There was help offered, success shown, and an out-stretched hand. What stood in their way? What's standing in your way of rising out of the pool of average?

Insecurity can be defined as a lack of confidence. We don't trust ourselves and create false imaginations of uncertainty. A false reality is created in our mind and we meditate on worse case scenarios. This can develop a lack of trust in ourselves, and others. Therefore, what starts off as excitement for a new opportunity is quickly uprooted by insecurity.

I've heard, "I know somebody like you can do it but ..." or "I can't see myself doing that." Their insecure voice is screaming and holding them back. If nothing changes, nothing changes. You will live a life that's consistent with the way you see yourself. Your income is the direct reflection of your self-image.

```
Tips to Getting Rid of Insecurity
```

Identify Your Insecurities

Take some time to write down what you are insecure about and the root cause. Some of your insecurities may stem from your childhood.

Break Old Habits

You should not only stop the bad habits but replace them with good ones that support your goals and objectives.

Mute the Critic

Turn off the voice in your head that is holding you back. Question what your inner voice is saying and decide if it is telling you the truth, what you want to believe, or makes you feel safe. I find using positive self-talk is helpful.

Stop Comparing Yourself to Others

This is one of the major obstacles in someone not overcoming their insecurities. Commit to be the best you that you can be and doing the best in every situation.

Develop Your Thinking

Commit to personal growth by reading positive books and listening to inspirational audios. Make it a daily habit.

Accept Yourself

Know what you can change about yourself, and what you can't. Then work on what can be changed.

Reflect on Past Successes

Some people find it helpful to journal past successes so they can review them in times of insecurity.

Removing insecurities is an ongoing process. I know, because I have had to work on it myself. In fact, I was the poster boy for insecurity. I did so many stupid things to try to mask or satisfy my past insecurities that most people would wonder how I made it this far if they knew. Over time, my self-confidence was developed, and some of the things I dealt with were slowly replaced with positive successes. I've always considered myself to have an entrepreneurial mind and knew that if I was to succeed, I would need to change and overcome. I am hoping more people can see that they may need to do this too.

3. Inadequacy

Have you ever thought, "I don't have what it takes?" Well, I have... more than once. Having my first child, starting graduate school, landing a corporate position, etc. I forgot that I had the education and experience for the situation. Maybe I didn't think I was good enough, or thoughts of past failures came back to haunt me.

How do we get over this to move up and forward? To recognize this voice and to turn it off, we first must know where the thoughts and feelings of inadequacy come from.

> **Our Past**: Feelings of inadequacy can come from our past. It could be from our parents, abuse, or other life situations. Our brains have been programmed with neural pathways created with the idea that, "I'm not good enough."

> **Associations**: The feeling of inadequacy can also come from our association. Who are you hanging around with? Are they lifting you up, or pulling you back down into the pool of mediocrity?

> **Failures**: The only way not to fail, is to not try to begin with. I learned that *having* a failure is different than *being* a failure, and you don't really fail unless you quit.

So, once we have recognized where feelings of inadequacy come from, what can we do to overcome it?

- ✓ Find a mentor or partner who uplifts, encourages and supports you.

- ✓ Use positive affirmation. I am a big proponent of this. The person who we listen to the most is ourselves. Speak how you should feel, how you want to see yourself, and your positive possibilities!

- ✓ Become more confident by dressing sharper, exercising, or thinking about someone you see as a confident person and taking on those attributes. Pretty soon those attributes will become a part of you.

- ✓ Stop comparing yourself to others!!! You will always feel bad when you compare someone else's strengths to your weaknesses. I guarantee you have strengths that they don't have, and they are probably secretly thinking you are better than them when they look at you.

- ✓ Know where you came from. Fair Warning…! This one expresses my thoughts as being a Christian. You are free to believe what you want, but I believe that there is a loving God, He made me, and He is always for me, not against me. "I can do all things through Christ who strengthens me."[7]

4. Negativity

Many times, as you are stepping into a new arena of life it will be necessary to change who you associate with. Water seeks its own level and we all become the sum of the five people we surround ourselves with. Are the people you are around talking about the negative of where you are, or the positive of where you can be? As I began my journey in creating multiple streams of income, I quickly found out that I had more acquaintances then actual friends. Some of my so-called "friends" felt challenged that I was thinking differently and wanted to invest my time into doing something different, so they gave me a hard time when I

---

7. Philippians 4:13

wanted to associate with other ambitious people. My ambition shined a spotlight on their laziness, and they tried holding me back.

Negativity can come from all sides. I had many people throw negative at me when I began to step out and act on my ambition and odds are you will too. In fact, if you don't have critics, then you aren't doing anything that's worth taking notice of.

There are 5 reasons someone is negative about what you are doing:

1. You are making them look bad. You are shining a spotlight on their laziness.
2. Others are either envious of your success, or embarrassed that they aren't doing anything themselves.
3. Seeing you moving forward makes them feel inadequate.
4. They've tried to reach for their dreams in the past but failed and quit.
5. You make them question themselves and the decisions they've made.

---

5. Time Management

If you are going to be investing time outside of your job toward a business, managing your time is imperative for your success. Contrary to what most people believe we all have between 3-5 hours of unproductive time every day. Average, unambitious people come home from their work, read the newspaper or watch the news until it's dinner time, then settle in to watch their TV shows until the evening news comes on, then bed. Worse yet are adults who spend hours playing video games.

Successful people follow a calendar. They itemize their hours every day to make full use of their time. They also schedule time for their family, faith, self-education and time alone to think.

Using either a calendar on your phone, or better yet a physical calendar, take your day and work backwards. Start with committing the hours you are devoted to your job. Include the time you commute. Block-off your dinner and family time and the hours you usually sleep. Now you will see what hours you have left to invest toward a side-business. Finally, you want to take this time and itemize it as to what you will be doing when. A good trick is to write some goals you want to reach by the end of each week. Having great time management also will keep you from getting distracted. When you're smart with your time management you won't waste your time or be unproductive. Take an evaluation of your daily habits, how you use your time. Making time is different than finding time. Place the same commitment into your side-business that you do for your job.

PART SIX

Sidepreneur: Where to Start

I've had many people tell me that they want to create another income stream on the side of their job, but don't know where to start. They tell me they don't have any good ideas.

The good news is that you don't have to have a world-changing idea. There are countless opportunities available. You just need to identify the best opportunity for you. A single spark of an idea can be worth millions.

Step One: Research and Explore

There are too many opportunities for a side business for me to list them all. Start by deciding what your long-term goal or vision is and if you want a side-business that creates an active/linear income or a passive, ongoing income.

Linear Income:	Passive/Ongoing Income:
A linear income is where you are trading your hours for dollars. The income stops when you stop working. In order to make money in linear income you must keep recreating the process.	A passive or ongoing income is just as it sounds, it's an income where you do work once, but continue getting paid from it on an ongoing basis. You don't need to keep recreating the process.
Examples: a job, self-employment	*Examples: investing, real estate, publishing, network marketing, etc.*

Once you have decided what type of income stream you want to create, you should decide what industry you want to be in, who you want to serve. What's the competition like in that industry and are there opportunities that you want to be in? Take an assessment of where the industry may be heading in the future and if you can capitalize on it. For example, if you are wanting to repair VCRs, DVD players and TVs on the weekends, you may not have much, if any business. However, if you learn to repair screens on tablets, cell phones and hand-held games, you will find there is a need for that and will be able to make some money.

Step Two: Choose a Niche

The riches are in the niches. A mistake many people make who are wanting to go into business for themselves is to start a business with too broad a target market. Just like in medicine, a specialist gets paid more and is in more demand than a general practitioner. First, choose the industry you want to have a business in. Then, narrow the industry to a specific target market. Finally, narrow your target market down to a smaller niche. I've provided a free tool called, "Finding Your Niche Worksheet" at www.sidepreneurbook.com/resources.

EXAMPLES

Industry	Target Market	Niche
Pest Control ⇨	Residential Pest Control ⇨	Mosquito Control
Real Estate ⇨	Flipping Houses ⇨	Flipping Houses on eBay
Fashion Design ⇨	Custom Designed Socks for Men ⇨	Sock Subscription Boxes through Amazon

Step Three: Find a System or Mentor

Most people think that success is difficult. It's not, it's simple. You just need to know the right success principles. The problem most people have is that they don't know where to find those principles. You can learn success principles through audios and books, but the best place is through another person who has been successful in the area you are pursuing.

One of the most important keys to anyone's success, not just in business, but in your spiritual life, parenting, marriage, etc. is having a coach or mentor; someone that has an interest in your success. Most people skip this important step because they don't believe they need a mentor.

Mentorship dates to a poem written by Homer in 800 BCE called, *The Odyssey*. In this classic poem, "mentor" was used by a character who was assigned to be a teacher and advisor to Odysseus's son. Since that time, mentors have played a role in teaching philosophy or teaching a trade or skill.

If one chooses not to use a mentor, they are then forced to figure everything out themselves; trial and error. Having a mentor gives you access to someone that has at least some of the knowledge that you seek or need and the experience to direct you around unnecessary mistakes you could make.

So, if you understand the importance of having a mentor, what should you look for in a coach and mentor?

> ### *A Good Mentor Should...*

Council: A mentor is there to listen to you and guide you along the path you are wanting to go. They are not there to make life decisions for you or give you all the answers, but to be another party that can provide you with a different viewpoint.

Consult: Mentors are there to provide you with their insight and experience. They see from a higher vantage point because they've already walked the path you are going down, and they guide you through the journey. This can save you time, money, headaches and resources.

Cheerlead: Mentors are your biggest cheerleader. They applaud you in the good times and support, encourage and lift you up in the bad. They have your back. When mistakes or setbacks are made, they help you to see the lessons to be learned, pick you up, dust you off so you can start again.

But you as a mentee also have responsibilities in the mentor-mentee relationship. It shouldn't be one-sided.

A Good Mentee Should...

Communicate: It's not the mentor's responsibility to be reaching out to you as the mentee. Be the one to take initiative in reaching out to the mentor. Be respectful of their time and coordinate a time that is convenient to your mentor's schedule.

Be Honest: Just as a doctor can't give an accurate diagnosis if the patient doesn't provide all the symptoms, a mentor can't give accurate advice or counseling if the mentee is not honest with them. You must be open and honest with the information you provide.

Trust: You chose your mentor for a reason. It's important that you trust them and what they are telling you. Trust goes both ways. The mentor needs to be able to trust you as the mentee in that you are providing them with truthful information on your end and that you are taking and applying their advice and counseling. In addition, there needs to be an atmosphere of confidentiality between the mentor and the mentee.

Step Four: Plan your Work

Planning before you begin acting will save you time and energy in the long run. It will also help you in making sure you are covering all your bases, especially when it comes to your legalities. Do you need to set up a legal entity? Will you need licenses or permits? These are some of the questions you need to answer before you begin. Developing a business plan and a profit and loss statement are also important documents a Sidepreneur should have. Taking time to create these will help you know how much money you may need to invest as well as the time commitment you may need to allot. Failing to plan can cause your plan to fail.

Step Five: Work your Plan

Eventually there comes a time when you need to act. Some people get stuck in the planning phase and never move forward. Just as you don't want to fly off the seat of your pants, you can also make the mistake of over-planning and wanting to work out every detail. Dr. David Schwartz in his book, *The Magic of Thinking Big* calls this having "Detailitis". You can get frozen on starting because you feel like you don't have all the information. There comes a time when you must decide you have the vital pieces of information you need to get started, and then begin.

PART SEVEN **Don't Burn Any Bridges**

1. Give 100%

I want to take the time to stress that it's important, as you begin and continue as a Sidepreneur that you stay true to you commitment as an employee and give 100% of you time and focus during your working hours to your employer. It can be very easy to get caught-up in using company time for your side-business endeavor. I know, because I've been there myself. I get more excited about having a business on the side and the opportunity that it starts to consume my thoughts and they can, if not watched creep into my time for my job.

Be a good example as well as a loyal employee and continue to give your employer your 100%. You may not like what you are doing for a job, but you accepted it. Also consider yourself fortunate that you have a steady income while you are pursuing your own business on the side. Not only does it provide you with an income and healthcare, but it takes the pressure off you to have to make an immediate income from your side-business. Remember, we are not talking about getting-rich-quick. Having an income from a job also provides you with the money you will need to get your business up and going.

So, don't jeopardize your job while you are a Sidepreneur. Just as you should be giving 100% to your family at home, give 100% to your job during your committed working hours. If you lost your job because you are doing personal work you will frustrate your finances, your family, and may even lose the support of those you love. It also gives a bad reputation to whatever it is you are choosing to do. After you clock out for the day, then it's YOUR TIME!

2. Not Everyone is Like You

Be careful who you share your ambitions and dreams with; this includes posting about it on social media. Not everybody thinks like you or will be as excited as you are. I've heard of situations where someone shared their ambition of a side-business to a co-worker at their job in the breakroom only to have their co-worker go behind their back and use it against them with their supervisor causing them to lose their job.

Unfortunately, there are many people who enjoy tearing other people down. They resent seeing others succeed. You can argue with people who are negative or don't have ambition, but in the end, you are wasting your time. Yes, you could tell them what you really think about them, but success is the greatest revenge. Once you become successful in the business you are working toward, some of those people may become your biggest cheerleader.

CONCLUSION

In the past, moonlighting was considered unconventional, and even somewhat secretive doing something behind the backs of the employer. Jobs were careers where employees stayed 30-40 years in a stable position receiving a pension upon retirement. Well, times have certainly changed. The average time for someone working in a position is 2-4 years and pensions are a rare find. If you ask, you'll probably find that 5 out of 10 people are doing something on the side of their full-time job for another income. Some are in business for themselves, but most are working a second job.

This book was written for those people who what to go somewhere in their life by becoming a Sidepreneur, an entrepreneur on the side. They are tired of being average and want to have more, do more and be more. It was intended to help the winner inside of you to rise and provide a path for you to take yourself to a new level. The amount of money we make determines the options we have in life and the quality of life we live now, but especially in our later years. Why not take a few hours of your unproductive time each day and invest it into a business of your own? Creating multiple streams of income can bring you more money, more time and more options.

Take advantage of the resources associated with this book at www. sidepreneurbook.com. They were made for YOU. Imagine how your life can be different 5 years from now. But you MUST take action! Don't let this be just another book you read. Take your life and future seriously. Every day that goes by is a day we can't get back. I believe that you were made for greatness. You are not an accident. You have what it takes to not only change your life, but the lives of future generations. If you change the way you think, you will change your life.

Go Make it Happen!

> **"Sometimes I get lost in my own world.**
> **That's okay, they know me there."**
> —Rik Covalinski

BONUS ONE The Ten Traps of Average

1. Waiting Until You Have All the Information

When I began looking for an opportunity, I began reading books and turned to the Internet as you probably did. I was quickly over-saturated with multiple ways to create a side-income. It seemed like everyone had their own magic way of making money, books to read, classes to take and webinars to watch. I quickly found myself so focused on getting information on what opportunities were out there and how others were succeeding in their opportunity that it took me years before I realized the most important thing to do was to START! Start where you are and blaze a trail forward.

I remembered when I was in my 20's and decided to start a professional educational touring theatre company. I returned home from living the life of an actor and said to myself, "I'm going to start a business." I didn't know anything about business, marketing or how to get started. But I just started. It was a lot of trial and error. The problem was when it was an error, I lost money and it was MY money. I was successful at it for a couple of years, but decided I wanted to learn more about business and went to graduate school.

2. Waiting for the Perfect Timing

I was told by a mentor that my life is the slowest it will ever be. Every month, every week, in fact every day my life gets busier. Too many use the excuse that they have too much going on in their lives to start something on the side. There are some legitimate reasons to temporarily delay, but if you are waiting for everything in your life to be perfect, it will never happen.

People find time to do the things they want to do. Your investment is your inconvenience. But, when you invest inconvenience, you get back convenience. There will never be the perfect time to start. You just need to start. Doing it now is more important than doing it perfectly.

3. Information Constipation

Have you ever had information constipation? It's where you have had your mind filled with so much information and details you can't get started on anything. With the Internet you have access to a world of information. This can be good, and bad. There's no shortage of people offering you their "proven system" or "free webinar" and you can quickly find yourself spending all of your time chasing information and you never get started. It's like drinking from a firehose. You try to get started but get overloaded and never do.

Set a window of time to explore and research your opportunity options and choose your top three. Look into the effort, time, money, commitment and competition of those top three and choose the right niche for you and get started.

I've provided a free tool called, "Finding My Niche Worksheet" at www.sidepreneurbook.com/resources.

4. Chasing Rabbits

Yes, there are a lot of choices for opportunities that you can have on the side of your job. I recommend that you do a little homework before you type, "side-line business opportunities" into a search engine. There are limitless opportunities in the world today and you can become easily distracted with the next big idea that you see or the next "must attend webinar" that is advertised.

Decide on your niche and stick to it. You can't do everything at once. Take note of the interesting opportunities you see or hear of, but work on one thing at a time. Once you've found success at your niche, then it can be a good time to review other possibilities and pursue them, or better yet incorporate them into what you are already doing.

For example, if your niche is making an Internet-based course you will come across the opportunities of recording an audio book, self-publishing, selling your course using affiliate marketing, marketing yourself for speaking engagements, and the list will go on. I think it's a great idea to have a file where you keep ideas and other opportunities and add as you go, but not try to do everything at one time. It will be like chasing rabbits. If you try to catch all the rabbits at one time, you won't catch any. But if you identify one rabbit and catch it, then you can move onto a second, a third and so forth.

5. Procrastination

3 turtles were sitting on a log and 2 decided to jump. How many turtles are left on the log? The answer...... 3! Why? Because they only THOUGHT about jumping. You can think about doing something all you want, but until you get up and actually do it, it won't happen.

> **Procrastination happens when we:**
> 1. *Don't value time*
> 2. *Are undisciplined*
> 3. *Don't prioritize our time*

Overcome procrastination by planning your day, making a list of what you want to get done or achieve each day and following through with doing it. Decide that you won't enjoy ___X___ until you finish doing ___Y___. When you begin to get things marked off your list you will feel better about yourself knowing you got something accomplished.

6. Distractions

Life is full of distractions. Distractions are more prevalent than they ever were with the Internet, cell phones, social media, gaming, TV, email, etc. Decide to block, or better yet cut out your distractions.

> ### *Quick Tips on Removing Distractions*

Turn Off Digital Distractions: Shut off your cell phone and social media for set periods of time during the day so you can focus on the task at hand. If you don't have the discipline to do this on your own, there are apps available that can help you take charge of your digital distractions.

Schedule Your Day: Have a calendar that you use to schedule your time and follow it. Block out the times you plan to work on your side-business, review it every evening before going to bed and again in the morning. Decide to follow your daily schedule and follow it.

Minimize Negativity: There are plenty of negative people who, if allowed, will drain your time and energy. They either have a victim mentality or are seemingly always pessimistic and enjoy bringing others into their negative world. Don't let these people steal your time. Remember that you become who you hang around.

Take Frequent Breaks: It's easy to let our minds drift off. As a Sidepreneur you've already spent the better part of your day at a job. Thoughts of what needs to get done around the house, what you need to do at your job tomorrow, family conflicts and financial strains can quickly creep into your mind causing you to become unfocused. Give yourself frequent breaks and make sure you are scheduling some time for yourself.

Distractions can cause us to waste time. If you are going to be investing your time outside of your job and family time toward a side-business, make sure you are not wasting it by just being busy. Make that time as productive as you can. By avoiding distractions and focusing your time you will find you are using less time in the long run.

7. Excuses, Excuses, Excuses

Average people have an excuse for everything; why they can't, shouldn't or couldn't. That's why they will never be more than average. Excuses tend to always blame external circumstances. Making excuses become a habit and form an average person's reality. To them, it justifies why things aren't going their way to make them feel better.

> ### 3 Ways You Can Remove Excuses

Change Your Vocabulary: Remove excuse vocabulary such as, "But..." This automatically puts up a roadblock in your mind. Replace the, "But..." with, "How can I...?". Be solution focused not problem focused.

Walk Through Your Fears: Excuses are used when we have a fear of trying something new or getting out of our comfort zone. Thinking about the fears are worse than doing what it is you are afraid of. Take action and do what it is you are afraid of. Action cures fear. It won't be as bad as you imagined it would be.

Create a New Routine: Excuses are founded in our habits. It's not easy breaking our habits. You will have to make a conscious effort in doing something new over a period of time to change the habits that are you are using as an excuse into positive supportive ones. Remember your excuses are holding you back. Own them and then decide to break free of them.

8. Looking at Past Failures

Average people think, "I should have..." or "I wish I would of...". You can't move forward if you continue to look behind you. If you are always looking in your rear-view mirror while driving, you will crash. We can't change the past; we can only learn from it. Regret is one of the thieves of life.

Failure isn't defeat unless you quit. Don't dwell on your past failures but use them as a lesson. Learn from them and move on. Ask yourself, "what could I have done differently?" or "what can I do next time instead?" Take an inventory of your successes and what you have done right. Our failures don't define us as a person. Don't live in the mistakes of yesterday, but in the spotlight of tomorrow.

9. Avoiding Risk

Average people avoid risks. Successful people take risks, but they are calculated risks. There is a difference in taking a risk versus being reckless. Successful people understand that there is a chance of failure, but that's okay. Failure is a part of success. If you never fail at something, that means you aren't trying or taking any risks. No one that achieved any success has avoided failure, or on the other hand blindly jumped into something without understanding what risk might be involved. Failure isn't final unless you quit.

Realize if you are going to move forward, there will always be some sort of risk. Risk isn't always financial. It could be a risk to your self-image, ego or getting out of your comfort zone. Risk requires us to have the courage to face the fear of uncertainty. We grow through the process and become more creative and confident.

10. No Money for a Startup

One of the top traps of an average person is thinking that they must have a lot of money to get started in a side-business. Yes, it will take some type of financial investment, but many opportunities can be started with little money. Growing up we were told, "It takes money to make money." There is truth to this if you are wanting to venture into investments, real estate, or buying into a franchise. Many small businesses like Amazon, Microsoft and Apple started out of a garage or basement. Many times, this is just used as an excuse.

In less than 24hrs one can open an online store selling crafts through Shopify, Facebook, Etsy, eBay or Amazon for only the cost of materials and monthly membership fee, join a network marketing business for $100-$200 and operate it on a shoestring budget, or write a book and self-publish it on the Internet. The days of having to buy or set up a brick and mortar store are over.

BONUS TWO

10 Sidepreneur Businesses You Can Start Today to Create an Ongoing Income Stream

Don't start by asking "how can I make more money" but look for people's problems and ask, "how can I solve their problem?". Opportunity can never be lost because opportunity is created. Look for an opportunity in everything!

Passive, Ongoing Income Streams

1. **Information Marketing:** You have knowledge and experience that others would be willing to pay for. Sell what you know through courses, workbooks and online learning platforms.

   Online Courses   *How-to Videos*

   Worksheets   *Workbooks*

   Audio Courses

2. **Build and Maintain Websites:** Almost every business understands the importance of having a website. They either don't have the knowledge or the time to make and maintain one themselves. As a website designer you can charge a monthly maintenance fee for websites you design.

3. **Social Media Manager:** With the need for businesses to have a presence on social media many small businesses are finding themselves without the knowledge or staff to manage their social media. You can have a monthly contract to manage the social media accounts for small businesses.

4. **Network Marketing:** Use a proven business system to duplicate your time, build a team and sell products. Network Marketing is unconventional, but so is making an extra $50,000 on the side. With the right parent company and education support system, more people are choosing this route to their financial freedom.

   It should be noted that one should do their due diligence and be cautious before partnering with a network marketing company. Being cautious is different than being skeptical. As with any opportunity do your research through credible sources such as the Better Business Bureau (BBB), Dunn and Bradstreet or the Federal Trade Commission. As with anything, doing a broad search through Google is not proper, credible research and will result in getting the opinions of others over actual facts. Be careful whose advice you are taking.

5. **Publish a Book:** In the past, publishing a book was difficult to do. Would-be authors would have to send their manuscript to multiple literary agents in the hopes one chooses to publish their book. Now, the Internet has given anyone who wants to publish a book an avenue to do so through self-publishing, or simply selling digital copies through Amazon, Nook, etc. You can earn monthly royalties from the sales of your book.

6. **Subscription Boxes:** Subscription boxes began in the early 2000's but have recently taken off. They are simply a box containing a product, or an assortment of products that customers purchase on a monthly subscription basis. New products are sent each month to the subscribers.

7. **Home Services:** These types of services can be set up on a weekly or monthly recurring contract. Having this type of contract will not

only provide you with income from ongoing accounts but gives homeowners a peace of mind and most likely a discount.

Pest Control	*Home and Business Cleaning*
Lawn Service	*Pet-sitting*
Holiday Decorating	*House-sitting*

8. **Sell Photos or Writings:** If you are creative and can take excellent photographs or are great at writing, consider selling your photos, greeting cards or writings online. You can sell them through your website, or through an e-commerce platform. Either way you will be able to sell multiple copies of one photo or piece of writing giving you an ongoing income from it.

9. **Affiliate Marketing:** If you don't have a product yourself and don't want to deal with shipping or drop shipping, you can sell other people's products as an affiliate marketer. Other people or businesses will pay you for the number of products you sell for them.

10. **Be a Consultant:** If you are an expert in a field consider being a consultant. You can troubleshoot, provide advice or improve performance to businesses or individuals. Create an ongoing income stream by placing them on a retainer and monthly contract.